YOU DON'T KNOW JACK®
THE BOOK

BERKELEY
SYSTEMS

RUNNING PRESS
PHILADELPHIA · LONDON

9 8 7 6 5 4 3 2 1
Digit on the right indicates the number of this printing

Library of Congress Cataloging-in-Publication Number 98-65175

ISBN 0-7624-0374-8

Jellyvision Editor: David Nathanielsz
Lead Writer: Steven Heinrich
Questions Written By: The Jellyvision Writers

Designed by Frances J. Soo Ping Chow
Edited by Brendan Cahill
Typography: Franklin Gothic and Coronet MT

This book may be ordered by mail from the publisher. Please include $2.50 for postage and handling.
But try your bookstore first!

Running Press Book Publishers
125 South Twenty-second Street
Philadelphia, Pennsylvania 19103-4399

Contents

Introduction 4

Game 1 8

Game 2 20

Game 3 32

Game 4 44

Game 5 56

Game 6 68

Game 7 80

Game 8 92

Game 9 104

Game 10 116

Introduction

Let's talk about you. You want to play. You're excited. Your bladder is as unstable as a deranged puppy out of medication. You're a trivia machine, and you're ready to produce.

Just settle down, Skippy. First you've got to know the rules.

QUESTION TYPES

This book is divided into several 10-question games, which you can play by yourself or with a group. Each game features four question types: Multiple-Choice, DisOrDat, Gibberish, and Jack Attack.

Multiple-Choice Questions There are seven Multiple-Choice questions in each game. They look something like this:

In a school for bears, which student would get at least a "B-" average?
A. Gentle Ben™   **C. Yogi Bear™**
B. Barney Bear™   **D. Smokey the Bear™**

The answer to this would be "C," because Yogi is "smarter than the average bear." See how that works? The answers to Multiple-Choice Questions can be found by turning the page. It's quicker than going to the library to look it up yourself.

The Gibberish Question There's one Gibberish question in each game. The Gibberish phrase is a random series of words that rhyme with a well-known phrase. For example:

What common phrase does this rhyme with?
The fiddle nerd sold pee.

You'll find the real phrase on the next page. In this case, the answer is: *A little bird told me.*

We'll give you a few hints to help you out, but no multiple-choice answers. Got it? Super.

The DisOrDat Question In each game, there is a seven-point DisOrDat question. Take a look at this:

Below are seven Italian names. For each one, identify if it's a pasta or the name of an Italian opera composer.

1. Puccini 5. Rossini
2. Tortellini 6. Verdi
3. Rotini 7. Cavatelli
4. Penne

You just decide if it's one or the other. In this case, Tortellini, Rotini, Penne, and Cavatelli are pastas; Puccini, Rossini, and Verdi are opera composers. The answers to DisOrDats are found at the end of each game.

In some DisOrDats, one answer fits both of the categories. If there are going to be some answers that are "both," we'll let you know at the beginning. We're just nice that way.

The Jack Attack At the end of each game there is a Jack Attack. For each Jack Attack, you want to correctly match the root words with the corresponding matching phrase. The correct matches should be based on the category on the top of the page.

For example, if your Jack Attack clue is **Hangin' with the Wee Folk,** you might see **Gulliver** and match him with **Lilliputians.** You'd be right, and that'd be just swell. But then you might see **Dorothy** and match her with **Toto.** Then you'd be wrong, and you'd feel stupid. Yes, Dorothy had a dog named Toto, but you have to remember the category. In this case, the correct match would be **Munchkins.**

Jack Attack answers are found at the end of each game.

SCORING

Whether you're playing by yourself or with a group of people, the best way to play "You Don't Know Jack" is competitively. So we've provided you with an easy-to-learn scoring system. If you're playing competitively, it's best to have paper and pencils handy for scoring. It's even better if you all get inside a big steel cage and lock the door.

- Each **Multiple-Choice Question** is worth two points.
- **DisOrDats** are worth a total of seven points. For each DisOrDat question you get right, you give yourself one point. And a little love.
- The **Gibberish Question**. If you can figure out the Gibberish phrase without the help of a hint, you get four points. If you need one hint, take three points. Two hints, two points. Using all three hints gets you a single point. And if you still

can't figure it out after all the hints, you get nothing. Nada. Zilch.

- In the **Jack Attack,** each correctly paired root and match is worth two points. That's a total of 14 points, which means if you really stink at all the other questions, you can still feel like you have a chance to win it all in the Jack Attack round. You don't, but it's still a nice feeling.

If you don't understand a question, skip it and never come back. It's just over your head and that's not going to change.

PLAYING WITH YOURSELF

If you can't figure out how to play this by yourself, perhaps you need a simpler hobby. Have you ever considered macramé?

Each game ends with a ratings chart. You can compare your score with the chart to find out just how stupid you are.

PLAYING WITH A GROUP

First, get a few friends together. At least one. If you can't do that, start working on your personality. Try to be a better listener. Don't be afraid to be vulnerable.

It's easiest if one person is host for each game, so pick one. We suggest choosing the most attractive person in the room. You're all going to be looking at the host for the next fifteen minutes, so it's best if he or she is not an eyesore.

Next, decide if you want to have individual players or teams. If you've got more than three players you should make teams. It's better that way. Trust us. The host should write the player or team names down on a sheet of paper. Each player/team should come up with a different "buzzer" sound. The human noises meant to represent barnyard animals work well as buzzer sounds, because they're easily distinguished. It's also an opportunity to realize how those noises sound nothing like the real animals.

For the Multiple-Choice questions the host should read off the category, the question and all Multiple-Choice answers. Host: Don't giggle while you do this. We spent a lot of time writing these questions so don't screw them up with your delivery.

As soon as the host is done reading, the players can buzz in by "mooing" or "clucking" or whatever it is, while frantically waving their arms. The host should take a minute to appreciate how idiotic they look, then call on the person who buzzed in first.

If they get it right, the host gives that player/team two points by drawing two chicken-scratch mark under their name. (That's right, chicken-scratch marks...

STUMPED?

then screw your neighbor!

If you don't know the answer to a Multiple-Choice question—or know that one of your opponents doesn't—you can buzz in, say "Screw 'Em" and force them to answer the question. If your opponent doesn't get the answer, they lose two points. If they get it right, they get two points and you lose two points. But remember, you can only screw on Multiple-Choice questions and you can only do it once per game, so screw wisely.

notice the barnyard metaphor is holding.)

If they miss it, we highly encourage taunting. Then, allow any of the other players to cluck in. And so on, until somebody gets it right. If no one gets it right, tell them the right answer and read the corresponding comments. Try to be funny while doing this; no one likes a boring game-show host.

For Gibberish questions, the host should read the category and the Gibberish phrase. If after five seconds nobody's buzzed in, the host should read the first clue for the idiot players. Every five seconds the host should read another clue. If nobody gets it after the final clue has been read then move on and nobody gets any points. Oh, and one person must die.* It's the rules. Don't question them.

For the DisOrDat every player or team should have a pencil and some paper. As the host reads the DisOrDat, the players should write down their responses to each of the seven items. After all seven have been read, players should pass their answers to the player or team to the right and the host can read the answers.

The Jack Attack is the final part of the game. Each player/team gets sixty seconds to view the Jack Attack page and write down the seven matches. The host can keep time by using a stopwatch, or stamping his or her foot like a horse sixty times. After all players/teams have had their turn, they again pass their answers to the right and the host reads the correct matches for the Jack Attack.

The host then totals up the points and announces the winner. Thumb wrestle to break any tie. No, wait—the two players should urinate in different parts of the room to mark off barnyard territory while making their clucking or mooing sounds, and then fight to the death! Yeah, that's it.

Finally, if you don't like these rules, change them. If you have an aversion to barnyard animals, imitate a choo-choo train. Really, we just don't care, because whatever you do, YOU DON'T KNOW JACK!

* **Don't actually kill someone, you sicko.**

Game

1

TWINKIES™
OLDER THAN CHRIST

If these foods were made on the birthdate of the historical figure on their labels, which one would have the OLDEST "born-on" date?

a snack cakes from Dolly Madison™

b frozen pizza from the Red Baron™

c beer from Samuel Adams™

d popcorn from Orville Redenbacher™

Hash-Slingin' Sculptures

If the famous statue called the Aphrodite of Melos applied for a waitressing position at Hooters™, what might prevent her from getting the job?

a.
She's shy about showing her skin.

b.
Her breasts are too big.

c.
She can't carry a tray properly.

d.
She loses her head with the customers.

Gibberish Question 3
Drinking & Bladder Control

With what classic childhood tune does this phrase rhyme?

Dinkle tinkled in a bar.

Hint 1
They're like diamonds in the sky.

Hint 2
But they aren't Lucy.

Hint 3
Get out your telescope for this song.

American revolutionary leader Sam Adams was born in 1722 and poured his last beer in 1803. And if you've opened his coffin lately, you'd agree that he has definitely skunked.

SHE CAN'T CARRY A TRAY PROPERLY. SHE'S GOT NO ARMS. BUT, ODDS ARE THAT IF HER SHIRT'S TIGHT ENOUGH, HOOTERS™ PATRONS WOULDN'T EVEN NOTICE.

Vacation Plans for Obsessive-Compulsives

You love to travel and are obsessed with hygiene products.
Which of the following is NOT actually something you can do?

(a) take a cruise to the Ivory™ Coast™

(b) climb the Lava™ flows of Camay™

(c) drink with Zest™ from an Irish Spring™

(d) stay home and listen to your Dial™ Tone™

Question 5
Revenge of the Birds

A flock of revenge-seeking turkeys knocks you down and makes a wish on you!
If they use your anatomical equivalent of a wishbone,
what will they rip out of your body?

a your humerus

b your coccyx

c your patella

d your clavicle

Question 6
Come Aboard, Torture's Waiting for You!

Suppose the Love Boat's Captain Stubing gets sick and tired of Gopher's antics
and decides to "keelhaul" him. How will Gopher be punished?

a. forced to sit naked on the poop deck

b. made to "walk the plank"

c. dragged under the ship from side to side

d. tied to the anchor

B. UNFORTUNATELY, YOU CAN'T CLIMB THE LAVA FLOWS OF CAMAY BECAUSE THERE'S NO SUCH PLACE AS CAMAY. BUT IF THERE WERE, IT WOULD BE THE MOST KISSABLY SOFT PLACE IN THE WHOLE WORLD.

The crazed fowl are gonna take your clavicle, or collarbone, which is roughly equivalent to a turkey's wishbone. That's pretty bad, but it's nothing compared to what they're going to do with the stuffing.

In order to "keelhaul" Gopher, Captain Stubing would have to drag him back and forth underneath the ship.

Hate . . . exciting and new.

Gimme a Kissy, Lurlene

**Let's say Richard Dawson travels back in time to 1873
to host the famous family feud between the Hatfields and the McCoys.
Which historical event should kick off the very first show?**

a. A Hatfield chops up a McCoy's still.

b. A McCoy elopes with a Hatfield's daughter.

c. A Hatfield wrecks a McCoy's new buggy.

d. A McCoy accuses a Hatfield of hog theft.

...And ThUS GoD SmOtE ANNOYinG CreATUrES

According to the Book of Genesis, on what day would God have rested if he had decided not to create Barney™?

a.
the first day

b.
the fourth day

c.
the sixth day

d.
the seventh day

I WAS A GRAMMAR SCHOOL JUNKIE

If you were actually "Hooked on Phonics™," what would you need to do for your next fix?

a.
write in shorthand

b.
learn the Greek alphabet

c.
spell words without vowels

d.
study the sounds of words

According to 100 surveyed historians, an accusation of hog theft started the feud. Of course, the show won't really kick off until Richard Dawson kisses all the Hatfield and McCoy women, and gets about a hundred bullets put in him.

On the sixth day God created all the creatures that walked upon the land. And on the seventh day, God put Satan in charge of television programming.

d. Phonics is the study of word sounds. But don't do it to yourself, man! Next you'll be getting wasted on linguistics. And then grammar. Before you know it, you'll be out on the street corner begging for a schwa.

Tough Yet Sensitive

Schwarzenegger Movie, Condom, or Both?

1. "Predator™"
2. "The Terminator™"

3. "Magnum™"

4. "Pumping Iron™"

5. "Red Heat™"

6. "Commando™"

7. "Rough Rider™"

That's What They Used To Call Me

1. Palestine

the Bible

"Alice"

3. Sugar Smacks™

Saudi Arabia

cereal

Nissan™

Toyota™

"Maude™"

4. Persia

Smacks™

June Bugs

Golden Crisp™

Crickets

Africa

Volkswagen™

7. Rhodesia

Dig 'Em

Hammer

Tanzania

"The Hogan Family"

2. The Silver Beatles

Sugar Bear™

Egypt

Middle East

he Artists Formerly Known as the Silver Beetles

Zimbabwe

Iran

The Beatles

5. Datsun™

"My Two Dads"

Israel

6. "Valerie"

Istanbul

DisOrDat Answers

1. Predator™/*movie*

2. The Terminator™/*movie*

3. Magnum™/*condom*

4. Pumping Iron™/*movie*

5. Red Heat™/*movie*

6. Commando™/*both*

7. Rough Rider™/*condom*

Jack Attack Answers

1. Palestine/Israel

2. The Silver Beatles/The Beatles

3. Sugar Smacks™/Smacks™

4. Persia/Iran

5. Datsun™/Nissan™

6. "Valerie"/"The Hogan Family"

7. Rhodesia/Zimbabwe

36 points or better: Okay.
Not completely idiotic.

30–35 points: Eh.
Some idiotic moments.

20–29 points: Pretty bad.
*This is about what we'd expect
an idiot to do.*

10–19 points: L'idiot.
That's French for "idiot."

0–9 points: You win!
*And if you scored this low,
you probably believe that.*

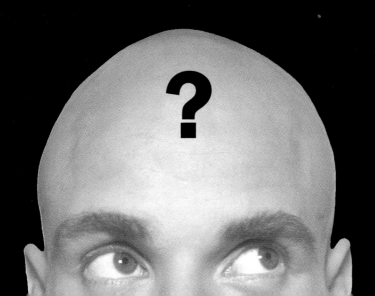

Game

Question 1
Dream On, Little Buddy!

**If Gilligan says that once the Minnow is repaired,
he'd like to sail around the "Islands of Langerhans,"
the Professor would tell him he'd have to be:**

a. on Mars

b. a character in "Gulliver's Travels"

c. microscopic

d. on Earth around three million B.C.

Question 2
Dirty Underwear
vs. Sexual Reproduction

**Choose the now-debunked scientific theory that this equation supports:
sweaty underclothes + wheat = mice**

a spontaneous generation

b biogenesis

c creationism

d deus ex machina

Question 3
A Beer! A Beer!
My Kingdom for a Beer!

**The year is 1419. Sir John Falstaff enters his favorite pub and wants to impress
his drinking buddies. How might he order a drink in iambic pentameter?**

a. "Excuse me, waiter, could I get a beer?"

b. "Forsooth, a beer if you please."

c. "Wench, a beer anon."

Answer 1

He'd have to be microscopic, because the Islands of Langerhans are in the pancreas. And tune in next week when Gilligan gets stranded on an uncharted desert testicle!

Answer 2

a. In centuries gone by it was common belief that living things spontaneously generated themselves from non-living things. One Belgian doctor thought that mice could be generated from sweaty clothes and wheat. Turns out you just get a bad episode of "Hee Haw."

Answer 3

"Excuse me, waiter, could I get a beer?" This is the only sentence with five feet, or word couplets, in which one syllable is short and the other is long. But by closing time, you can bet the Bard will be speaking in blank verse.

Question 4

HUNG LIKE A TROJAN HORSE

Which slang term for masturbation might the mythological character Odysseus assume was named in his honor?

a.
"choking the chicken"

b.
"rubbing the magic lamp"

c.
"battling the cyclops"

d.
"tuning the trouser trombone"

Question 5

ThE FiRst LaDY WaS Not the FiRst LAdY

Who is the only former U.S. President whose personal life could be re-enacted on "Divorce Court"?

a John F. Kennedy

b Jimmy Carter

c Ronald Reagan

d Richard Nixon

Gibberish Question 6
Tight-Asses & Oppositional Thinking

With what phrase does this rhyme?
Very scary tight-bun Barry

Hint 1
It's from a nursery rhyme.

Hint 2
In it, there's a girl who gardens.

Hint 3
How does her garden grow?

23

C

"battling the cyclops"
In Homer's "Odyssey,"
Odysseus kills the Cyclops by
driving a spear into its eye.
See, your mom was right.
It can make you blind.

C. UNCLE RONNIE IS THE ONLY U.S. PRESIDENT TO HAVE BEEN DIVORCED. AND SINCE HE WAS AN ACTOR, HE COULD DO THE "DIVORCE COURT" RE-ENACTMENT HIMSELF.

Answer 6: Gibberish Question

MaRy, MAry, QuitE CoNTraRY...

Now, what the hell are cockleshells . . . and why are they talking about them in a nursery rhyme?

Music Only a Dog Could Love

Complete this analogy:
Scooby Doo™ is to Scrappy Doo™ as accordion is to:

a. **Daphne**
b. **singer**
c. **concertina**
d. **Lawrence Welk**

Hollywood in the 16th Century

If each of the following had lived in Shakespeare's time, who would have MOST likely played Juliet in "Romeo and Juliet"?

a.
Julia Roberts

b.
Angela Lansbury

c.
both Olsen twins

d.
Keanu Reeves

GReeK MYthOLogy at the mAll

You want to take your buddy Achilles shopping for some new shoes before his next big battle. Knowing his weakness, which of the following will offer him the best protection?

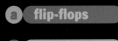
a flip-flops

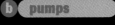
b pumps

c mules

d slingbacks

c. A concertina is a little accordion. Like Scrappy, it's a smaller and even more irritating version of the original.

Answer 8

In Shakespeare's time, all the roles were played by men and boys, so Keanu Reeves is the only possible choice. Isn't there just something horribly frightening about the phrase "Keanu Reeves is the only possible choice"?

Answer 9

b. Pumps would offer the most protection for Achilles' biggest weakness: his heel. Also, he should make sure his battle pack is stocked with plenty of nail polish in case he gets a run in his hose.

Play That Funky Music, Old White Man

Vice President, Funk Musician, or both?

1. Hannibal Hamlin

2. Spiro Agnew

3. Bootsy Collins

4. Walter Mondale

5. Sly Stone

6. George Clinton

7. James Brown

I Don't Know What It Is, but I'll Buy It!

soap

special sauce

car

mayonnaise

2. Folgers™

3. Chrysler Cordoba™

Cooling Sensates™   *Breathysin™*

sea monkeys

4. Rogaine™

toothpaste

fake strands of hair

coffee

sugar

flavor crystals

Doric leather

pumice

Scrubbing Bubbles™

alcohol

1. Certs™

stain remover

cup holder

molten rock

nougat

hummus

hidden cameras

Retsyn™

fine Corinthian leather

5. Dow™ Bath Cleaner

driver's side airbags

6. Big Mac™

Spain

7. Lava™

Minoxydil™

DisOrDat Answers

1. Hannibal Hamlin/*veep*

2. Spiro Agnew/*veep*

3. Bootsy Collins/*funk*

4. Walter Mondale/*veep*

5. Sly Stone/*funk*

6. George Clinton/*both*

7. James Brown/*funk*

Jack Attack Answers

1. Certs™/Retsyn™

2. Folgers™/flavor crystals

3. Chrysler Cordoba™/fine Corinthian leather

4. Rogaine™/Minoxydil™

5. Dow™ Bath Cleaner/Scrubbing Bubbles™

6. Big Mac™/special sauce

7. Lava™/pumice

Rate Your Score

36 points or better: Nice work.
*We'll call you "Mercurio," because
that sounds like a smart person.*

30–35 points: "Hardy."
*Because you're half mystery-solving
youth/half overweight comedian.*

20–29 points: You're "Doobie."
Accept it.

10–19 points: "Tess."
*It kind of rhymes with "ass,"
but not really.*

0–9 points: "Pauly."
Just "Pauly."

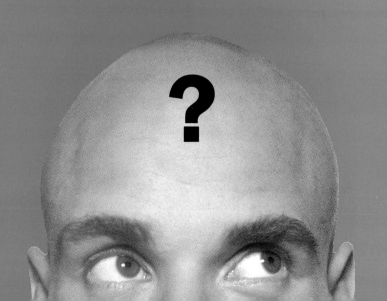

Game

A Very Brady Coronation

Imagine that Henry VIII marries Carol Brady instead of Catherine of Aragon. What is it about Carol that is similar to Catherine and will probably result in her beheading?

a.
She's suspiciously close friends with Alice.

b.
She's already been married.

c.
She bears only daughters.

d.
She wears bell-bottoms.

HisTOry LesSOn IN a whItE WIne SAuCe

Suppose Martha Stewart and Julia Child get together and reenact the Battle of the Five Forks. What war are they commemorating?

a.
World War II

b.
the Korean War

c.
the Franco-Prussian War

d.
the American Civil War

Gibberish Question 3

Pagan Headlines in Old Wales

With what product slogan does this phrase rhyme?

Celts in Poor South Shot in Sore Gland!

Hint 1
It's a slogan for a type of candy.

Hint 2
The candy is little, round and chocolatey.

Hint 3
You stay clean eating these.

Answer 1

C. KING HENRY GOT ANGRY WHEN CATHERINE OF ARAGON WOULDN'T GIVE HIM A SON. BUT IF CAROL LOSES HER HEAD, IT'LL AT LEAST GIVE MARCIA A LITTLE PERSPECTIVE ABOUT THAT SWOLLEN NOSE.

Answer 2

The Battle of the Five Forks was one of the last major battles of the Civil War. And let this be a lesson to you on proper war etiquette: the salad fork goes in the left eye; the dinner fork goes in the right eye. Use a moist linen napkin to wipe up the blood.

Gibberish Answer 3

MELTS IN YOUR MOUTH, NOT IN YOUR HAND.™

Just one more reason why M&M's™ are a better snack than a stick of butter.

'70s TV Families
& Their Interlopers

Complete this analogy:
Brady Bunch™ is to Oliver as Partridge Family™ is to:

a. Tracy
b. Reuben
c. Ricky
d. Chris

Question 5

The Periodic Table
& the House of Hanover

**If King George III and other rulers were really
made of "noble" stuff, which gas might they pass?**

a fluorine
b oxygen
c hydrogen
d neon

Question 6

Baked Goods & the Height-Challenged

The Keebler™ elves are what?

a nomadic
b carnivorous
c migratory
d arboreal

C. OLIVER AND RICKY. TWO SUPERFLUOUS CHILD CHARACTERS, TWO NEW CHILD STARS. FURTHER EXPERIMENTS IN THE BETTY FORD CLINIC'S "LET'S-SEE-IF-WE-CAN-GUARANTEE-FUTURE-CLIENTS" PLAN.

Answer 5

Neon is one of the six noble gases.
Now you know how the toilet came to be known as "the throne."

Answer 6

The Keebler™ elves are arboreal. They live in trees.
Although, when talking about those little punks, there are definitely
a lot of other words that come to mind before "arboreal."

On the Highway to Hell

Imagine that you're speeding your way through Europe, and you hit someone with your car. You don't have time to look at who you hit, so you just keep going.

You notice that as you go through Italy, people point and yell "Babbo Natale!" In France they cry "Père Noël!" and in Finland they scream "Ukko!" Who is plastered across your grill?

a. the Easter Bunny

b. Santa Claus

c. Baby New Year

d. Father Time

ToyS You waNT To ThrOW AGaiNst tHe WaLL

If the makers of Rubik's Cube™ were to branch out and make a Rubik's Dodecahedron™, how many colors would the new toy have?

a three

b seven

c ten

d twelve

She Married My Uncle in Vegas

Which of the following is NOT an antelope?

a. addax

b. affenpinscher

c. duiker

d. gemsbok

Better be on the lookout for pissed-off elves, because you just pulled a hit-and-run on Santa. That pretty much guarantees your spot on this year's "naughty list."

Answer 8

D. A DODECAHEDRON HAS TWELVE SIDES. BET IT'LL BE A REAL BITCH TELLING THE MAUVE SIDE FROM THE LAVENDER SIDE.

Answer 9

An affenpinscher is a dog. Which works out well, really. "Where the deer and the affenpinscher play" doesn't exactly roll off the tongue.

NBA™ Action Is Fantastnik!
NBA™ Player or Eastern European Leader?

1. Slobodan Milosevic

2. Arvydas Sabonis

3. Vlade Divac

4. Scottie Pippen

5. Milan Panic

6. Sasha Danilovich

7. Radovan Karadzic

You're Going on TV in That?

monogrammed sweater

1. Columbo

3. Corporal Klinger

coonskin cap

4. Gilligan

Skipper

jock strap

Shirley

6. Fonzie

smock

"Sit on it!"

trench coat

very angry

David Banner

mask

cigar

green

eye patch

sailor hat

bodkin

2. Davy Crockett

tunic

leather jacket

cowboy hat

ripped shirt

purple flip-flops

5. Laverne

"M*A*S*H™"

dress

baseball cap

khakis

7. The Hulk™

"Little Buddy"

leather & handcuffs

DisOrDat Answers

1. Slobodan Milosevic/*leader*

2. Arvydas Sabonis/*player*

3. Vlade Divac/*player*

4. Scottie Pippen/*player*

5. Milan Panic/*leader*

6. Sasha Danilovich/*player*

7. Radovan Karadzic/*leader*

Jack Attack Answers

36 points or better: Marcia Brady.
You're like the prettiest,
most popular one.

30–35 points: Greg Brady.
Not quite Marcia,
but your jeans are far out.

20–29 points: Sam the butcher.
Nothing overwhelming, just
a human being happy to be
surrounded by quality meat.

10–19 points: Cindy Brady.
Cute, but your answers are unintelligible.

0–9 points: Oliver.
When you arrive,
people know the end is near.

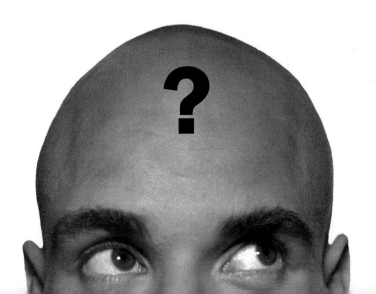

Game

4

The Health Benefits of Opera

Suppose listening to opera star Placido Domingo could actually cure the common cold.

If listening to an impostor sometimes created the same desired effect as listening to the real Placido Domingo, what would be the best name for this impostor?

a. Peabo Domingo
b. Placido Domingo
c. Placenta Domingo
d. Placebo Domingo

Question 2

IT'S A NICE PLACE TO VISIT, BUT...

Which of the following is NOT an actual place in the United States?

a. French Lick, Indiana
b. Big Bone Lick State Park, Kentucky
c. Big Beaver, Pennsylvania
d. Trout Lick, Kentucky

Question 3

SHuFflE-BoARd On IcE

If "The Karate Kid" wanted to become "The Curling Kid," what household task would Mr. Miyagi MOST appropriately force him to do?

a. pull hair out of the drain
b. sweep the floors
c. mow the lawn
d. put down the toilet seat

d. Placebo Domingo. A placebo, often a sugar pill, doesn't really do anything. The patient only thinks it does. Warning: Opera music may cause drowsiness. Do not operate heavy machinery while at the opera.

Answer 2

d. Trout Lick doesn't exist. In Kentucky, trout lick is an activity, not a location.

Answer 3

In curling, players use brooms to sweep the ice in front of a big sliding stone. Of course, the Curling Kid wouldn't really learn self-defense, he'd only be able to beat up "The Ice Capades™ Kid."

Question 4
Does It Glow in the Dark?

Say Demi Moore poses naked again for "Vanity Fair™," but this time, she covers herself completely in "tempera" paint. Which of the following would be true?

a. She'd have a chip on her shoulder.

b. She'd have a flea in her ear.

c. She'd have egg on her face.

d. She'd have mud in her eye.

Question 5
BetCha CAn't EaT JUst OnE

You're grilling up some foot-long human hot dogs. How many foot-long buns do you need to accommodate an average large intestine?

- ⓐ 5
- ⓑ 15
- ⓒ 23
- ⓓ 42

Gibberish Question 6
Mittens & Oscar Madison

With what saying does this phrase rhyme?
Make Miss Slob Hand glove grit.

Hint: 1
It's a song and a movie.

Hint: 2
It's about one's occupation.

Hint: 3
You might say it upon quitting your job.

Tempera paint is made using pigments, water and egg yolks, so Demi would have egg on her face. But, after "Striptease" and "The Scarlet Letter," she's probably used to it.

The large intestine is a mere 5 feet long. And they taste even better with a side of sphincter salad.

TAKe tHiS JoB aND SHOve IT

You may now turn your head and cough.

if I haD WAnTeD FEaTHErs On my ASS, I'd HaVE WORn A BoA

If Christopher Wren were in fact a wren, what might you expect to be true about him?

a. He wouldn't sing so much as scream.

b. He would do aerial reconnaissance.

c. He would build especially beautiful nests.

d. He would hang out with a teddy bear.

XYZ PDQ!

In the 1980s, if someone caught you with their SLR discussing the S&P with a CFO and reported you to the SEC, of what might you be accused?

a. sexual harassment

b. filibustering

c. espionage

d. insider trading

Fast Food Politics

Whom would you NEVER find in a town council meeting in McDonaldland™?

a. Mayor McCheese™

b. Grimace™

c. Hamburglar™

d. Sergeant McFry™

C. SIR CHRISTOPHER WREN WAS A FIRST-CLASS ARCHITECT, SO HE WOULD BUILD ESPECIALLY NICE NESTS. BET IT WOULD BE A BITCH DRAWING UP THE BLUEPRINTS.

Answer 8

Insider trading. Someone caught you talking
about the stock market with the Chief Financial Officer
and then ratted to the Securities and Exchange Commission.
Sure, you'll go to jail. A special jail. One of them
"ruthless" jails with a golf course and a croquet team.

Answer 9

There is no Sergeant McFry.
Rumor has it he was greased in 'Nam.

Breakfast Cereal & Biology

Animal on Box is a Mammal
or Not a Mammal?

1. Frosted Flakes™

2. Lucky Charms™

3. Sugar Smacks™

4. Rice Krispies™

5. Boo Berry™

6. Special K™

7. Quaker Oats™

Drink Me

1. Laverne DeFazio

philosophy

hemlock

yak's milk

Zima™

3. Homer Simpson™

blood

Marge

vodka martini

well water

urine

raw eggs

5. Radar O'Reilly

diet cola

Fresca™

Trapper John

milk & Pepsi™

Ovaltine™

Ripple™

Snapple™

secret agent

2. James Bond™

vampire

grape Nehi™

4. Socrates

orange juice & Coke™

choked on own vomit

scotch & soda

love

6. Dracula

boozehound

Lamont

7. Fred Sanford

Duff beer

1. **Frosted Flakes™**/*mammal*

2. **Lucky Charms™**/*mammal*

3. **Sugar Smacks™**/*not mammal*

4. **Rice Krispies™**/*mammal*

5. **Boo Berry™**/*not mammal*

6. **Special K™**/*not mammal*

7. **Quaker Oats™**/*mammal*

Jack Attack Answers

1. *Laverne DeFazio/***milk & Pepsi™**

2. *James Bond™/***vodka martini**

3. *Homer Simpson™/***Duff beer**

4. *Socrates/***hemlock**

5. *Radar O'Reilly/***grape Nehi™**

6. *Dracula/***blood**

7. *Fred Sanford/***Ripple™**

36 points or better: Succulent.
Much like a tasty Duck à l'Orange,
or Peking duck.

30–35 points: Mostly Juicy.
Like a good quiche, we think.
But we're not sure what quiche is.

20–29 points: Undercooked in parts.
Imagine microwaved fajitas.

10–19 points: Dry and raw.
Kind of like when they ate
the frozen dead people
in that "Alive" movie.

0–9 points: Rump roast.
As in you just got your ass fried.

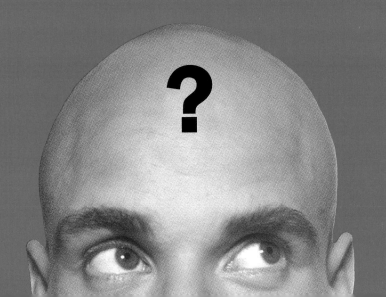

Game

FRiEd DouGH & ThE CLaSSiCS

You're going to the carnival with your buddy Narcissus. Given his little problem, where should you AVOID taking him?

a.
the Hall of Mirrors

b.
the Ferris wheel

c.
the Tilt-a-Whirl™

d.
the bumper cars

BETTER LIVING THROUGH CHEMICALS

Where would you most likely find ammonium lauryl sulfate?

a **in the shower**

b **at the beach**

c **in your body**

d **in the food pantry**

Gibberish Question 3
Just Don't Let Erwin near the Dam!

With what cliché does this phrase rhyme?
Flood! This dick Erwin brought 'er!

Hint 1
You say it about your relatives.

Hint 2
It's about the bodily fluids you and your relatives share.

Hint 3
How thick is your blood?

Answer 1

The Hall of Mirrors. Narcissus is famous for falling in love with his own reflection—he stared at it until he turned into a flower. And after falling in love in the Hall of Mirrors, you don't even want to know what he does with himself in the Tunnel of Love.

Answer 2

AMMONIUM LAURYL SULFATE IS A MAJOR INGREDIENT IN SHAMPOO. CHECK IT OUT NEXT WEEK...WHEN YOU BATHE.

answer 2:A
answer 2:A

Gibberish Answer 3

Blood is thicker than water.

Blood is thicker than water. And it's not as refreshing to drink, either.

Question 4
Shall I Compare Thee to an Uzi?

Suppose you're a bounty hunter tracking the narrator of Robert Frost's poem "The Road Not Taken" through the woods. Which road would you take to try to catch him?

a "the other one"

b "the one less traveled by"

c "the road by the babbling brook"

d "the road not taken"

Question 5
I Can't Get This Damn Song out of My Head

Suppose God had wanted to make Cain's life in exile even worse than it was. Considering Cain's punishment, which song would have been most appropriate to play over and over in his head?

a. The Cars' "Drive"

b. Dion's "The Wanderer"

c. Christopher Cross' "Sailing"

d. Kim Carnes' "Bette Davis Eyes"

Question 6
Your Passport to Life

You notice that on your birth certificate, your father signed the name "Allen Smithee." Judging by what this alias means in the film industry, what can you conclude about your father?

a. he doesn't want people to know he made you

b. he's actually a woman

c. he's primarily a maker of porn films

d. he wants you to be seen only late at night

59

b. Frost's poem reads: "Two roads diverged in a wood and I, I took the one less traveled by." And if you find that bastard, blow his brains out for ending his sentence with a preposition.

Answer 5

B. DION'S "THE WANDERER." CAIN WAS FORCED TO LEAVE THE FIELDS HE FARMED AND WANDER THE LAND. THIS, OF COURSE, IS THE BIBLE'S PARABLE FOR WHY GOD CREATED THE WALKMAN™.

Answer 6

Directors use the alias Allen Smithee
when they don't want folks to know who made the movie,
so your father probably doesn't want you to know
who made you. But you can still rent yourself out to other dads
for $1.99 an evening.

Question 7

Papa's Got a
Brand New Anchorman

Maybe America's best bet for president would be a mix of newsman Walter Cronkite and soul singer James Brown. Combining each one's famous nickname, what could you call a union of the two?

a. the Godfather of Objective News Reporting

b. the Grand Funkster of Sincerity

c. the Hardest-Working Trusted Man in America

d. Soul Brother of the Nightly News

Question 8

SEMITES & '70s MUSIC

Suppose a little Israeli boy is running around yelling for his father in Hebrew. Which musical group is likely to answer?

a Chic

b Abba™

c Queen

d Kiss™

Question 9

HOW cAN shE HaVE dE GaUlle?

Which of the following methods of birth control could best describe former French president Charles de Gaulle's approach to his nation's military involvement in NATO?

a. abstinence

b. the rhythm method

c. early withdrawal

d. entry with a latex condom

James Brown, "the hardest working man in show business," meets Walter Cronkite, once known as "the most trusted man in America."

"And that's the way it is . . . HAH!"

Abba is Hebrew for "Dad." It's also Swedish for "My name is Bjorn... come dance with me now."

De Gaulle pulled France out of NATO's military alliance. But you can bet NATO will be there to comfort France next time France gets screwed.

Cheese Gone Bad

Monster or Cheese?

1. Godzilla™

2. Gorgonzola™

3. Ebriah™

4. Asiago™

5. Rodan™

6. Grand Gouda™

7. Ghidrah™

Boy Meets Girl

1. **"Romeo & Juliet"**

Boy meets horse.

Boy meets giant shark.

Boy helps boy meet gir

boring play

Boy Wonder™

Girl meets girl.

my dog's name

4. **"Oedipus Rex"**

5. **"Cyrano de Bergerac"**

Boy meets showgirls.

Boy, oh, boy!

long nose

Boy eats boy.

7. **"Predator™"**

Boy makes robot.

Boy misses SATs.

plane crash

Buoy meets gull.

Boy meets alien.

2. "Personal Best"

Boy George

Boy meets Mom.

3. "Alive"

Boy meets steroids.

Boy loses sled.

Boy meets dragon.

Boy meets girl.

Orson Welles

Boy flosses girl.

pierced eyeballs

Boy gives girl cooties.

6. "Citizen Kane"

naked Hemingway

DisOrDat Answers

1. Godzilla™/*monster*

2. Gorgonzola/*cheese*

3. Ebriah™/*monster*

4. Asiago/*cheese*

5. Rodan™/*monster*

6. Grand Gouda/*cheese*

7. Ghidrah™/*monster*

Jack Attack Answers

1. *"Romeo & Juliet"/Boy meets girl.*

2. *"Personal Best"/Girl meets girl.*

3. *"Alive"/Boy eats boy.*

4. *"Oedipus Rex"/Boy meets Mom.*

5. *"Cyrano de Bergerac"/Boy helps boy meet girl.*

6. *"Citizen Kane"/Boy loses sled.*

7. *"Predator™"/Boy meets alien.*

Rate Your Score

36 points or better: Very Strong.
You could lift cinderblocks
with that brain.

30–35 points: Sorta shapely.
Do you own an Easyglider™?
You could use a little more exercise.

20–29 points: Thin.
We suggest you keep
your hat on at the beach.

10–19 points: Weak.
You've really let yourself go.

0–9 points: Flabby.
Call your local pharmacy.
They have drugs that can help you.

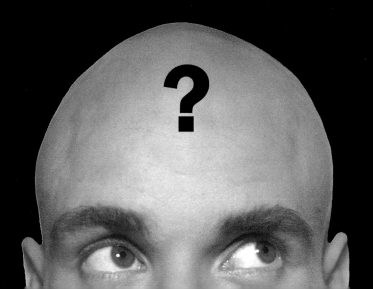

Game

6

Question 1

GettiNG wET iN HisTOry CLaSs

Suppose Marco Polo had played the kids' game "Marco Polo" to find his destination on his most famous exploration. If he yelled "Marco," which country would have yelled "Polo!" in return?

- a. Italy
- b. India
- c. China
- d. Australia

Question 2

MAYBE YOU SHOULD HAVE THAT LOOKED AT

If you walked into a phrenologist's office, which of the following would you be expected to remove?

a.
your shirt

b.
your pants

c.
your shoes

d.
your hat

Question 3

I Just Can't Find the Words...

Complete this analogy: "De Do Do Do, De Da Da Da" is to "That's all I want to say to you" as "Eep Opp Ork Ah-Ah" is to:

a. "See me, see you."
b. "What else is there for me to do?"
c. "That means I love you."
d. "I am Mork™ from Ork™."

Answer 1

Marco Polo spent 25 years exploring China. It must have been tough trying to get around that Great Wall with his eyes closed.

Answer 2

D. YOUR HAT. A PHRENOLOGIST STUDIES THE SHAPE AND "TOPOGRAPHY" OF YOUR HEAD AND THEN SUPPOSEDLY DECIPHERS YOUR PERSONALITY. WATCH IN AMAZEMENT AS HE CHECKS OUT YOUR FLAT HAIR AND DEDUCES THAT "YOU LIKE TO WEAR HATS."

Answer 3

In the song, "Eep Opp Ork" means "I love you."
"De Do Do Do," "Eep Opp Ork," "In-A-Gadda-Da-Vida"—who says they don't write songs like they used to?

Three Is a Magic Number

Which of these groups actually has three members?

a The Three Musketeers

b Three Dog Night

c The Three Stooges

d The Three Amigos

Question 5
Secretaries of the World, Unite!

If your secretary were a "secretary bird," how might you be killed if you asked it to work weekends and pick up your dry cleaning?

a. bitten in half

b. kicked to death

c. pecked through both eyes

d. sexually harassed to death

Question 6

Henry VIII & Frank Drebin

Of the following, which are there the most of?

a. Great Lakes

b. wives of Henry VIII

c. Ivy League schools

d. televised episodes of "Police Squad"

Answer 4

Dusty Bottoms, Lucky Day, and Ned Nederlander—The Three Amigos.
Coincidentally, three is also the number of minutes
they spent writing the script for that movie.

Answer 5

The secretary bird kicks its prey until it dies.
And then she takes care of all the funeral arrangements.

Answer 6

There are eight Ivy League schools. That's a lot of tweed.

Emergency Car Repair & Prosthetic Behinds

With what does this phrase rhyme?

Pin face of tire fake ass.

Hint 1
It's on a sign in buildings.

Hint 2
This is what you should do in an emergency.

Hint 3
Do it in the event of fire.

Question 8

Mary, Mary, Why You Druggin'?

Mary, Mary is quite contrary, and she's picked herself up a little drug habit as well.

If Mary devotes her entire garden to the growing of poppies, which of the following drugs can she NOT make from her harvest?

a.
opium

b.
cocaine

c.
morphine

d.
heroin

Question 9

THANKS FOR RUINING THE MOVIE FOR ME!

You're in a movie theater watching the 1980 bio-pic about John Merrick. If Mr. Merrick suddenly comes in and takes the seat in front of you, what might you think to yourself?

a. "This guy shows up late for everything!"

b. "Does he have to put his feet up like that?"

c. "Have a little popcorn with your butter!"

d. "Great, now I can't see the damn movie!"

IN CAse OF FiRE, BReAk GLasS.

And in case the extinguisher doesn't work . . . run like hell.

Answer 8

Unless Mary plants some coca plants she's not going to have any cocaine coming from her garden. She'll have to continue to get her cocaine from her supplier, Little Miss Muffet.

Answer 9

"Great, now I can't see the damn movie!" The movie you're watching is "The Elephant Man," the story of John Merrick—a Victorian circus freak with a huge, bulbous-shaped noggin. You might not be able to see the movie, but you could laugh really loud during all the sad parts.

O.U.I.—Operating Under the Influence

"Operation™" Game Piece or Liquor Drink?

1. Adam's Apple™

    2. Irish Eyes™

3. Funny Bone™

    4. Poop Deck™

5. Old Man's Milk™

    6. Water on the Knee™

    7. Charlie Horse™

It Only Sounds Dirty

1. Pandora's

Secret

pubic region

3. Black Hole of

Uranus

screw

hump

moist

4. Colossus of

great big boner

penis

one-bedroom apartment

Africa

box

my sock drawer

7. Archimedes'

Uncle Frank

Tootie

Rhodes

the great Louis Armstrong

2. Horn of

Satan

Damocles

tunnel

the Swordsman

longtime companion

Calcutta

Space

Newark

5. dowager's

pointy thing

Q-Tip™

6. sword of

Xena™

DisOrDat Answers

1. Adam's Apple™/*Operation*™

2. Irish Eyes/*drink*

3. Funny Bone™/*Operation*™

4. Poop Deck/*drink*

5. Old Man's Milk/*drink*

6. Water on the Knee™/*Operation*™

7. Charlie Horse™/*Operation*™

Jack Attack Answers

1. Pandora's/box

2. Horn of/Africa

3. Black Hole of/Calcutta

4. Colossus of/Rhodes

5. dowager's/hump

6. sword of/Damocles

7. Archimedes'/screw

36 points or better: Good job.
If you were a tree product,
you'd be rich maple syrup.

30–35 points: Decent.
More along the lines of
an attractive cedarwood door frame.

20–29 points: Nothing spectacular.
Like a pencil (not one of
those really good ones).

10–19 points: Not good.
Let's just call you "Woody."

0–9 points: Crappy.
Like toilet paper.

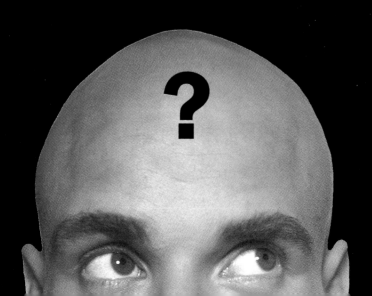

Game

Question 1

Monkeys & Spreadable Lunchmeat

The name SPAM™ is short for "spiced ham."
If a can of SPONKEY™ were to contain 100% spiced monkey, which ingredient could it NOT contain?

a. pure BARBARY APE extract

b. orange MARMOSET

c. bleached BONGO

d. hydrolyzed MACAQUE

Question 2

InteLLECtuAL MoveMENTS ThaT WiLL Give YOu a WHuPPinG

Which of the following would take place if you were brutalized by a proponent of "brutalism"?

a. A painter would beat you senseless.

b. An architect would kick your ass.

c. A philosopher would slap you silly.

d. A boxer would insult your poetry.

Gibberish Question 3

Give It to Opie, He'll Eat Anything

With what does this phrase rhyme?

Why Aunt Bee leave grits hot, mudder?

Hint 1
It's the name of a product.

Hint 2
You use it like margarine.

Hint 3
I can't believe you don't know it.

C

Bleached bongo would not be in SPONKEY™. Bongo would be in a can of SPANTELOPE™.

b. An architect would kick your ass. Brutalism was an architectural movement in the 1950s and '60s that included such features as bare cement and exposed ducts and pipes. The move-ment was named when the guy who wanted to call it "brutalism" beat the crap out of the guy who wanted to call it "lazy."

Gibberish Answer 3

I Can't Believe It's Not Butter™

Welcome Back, Homer

Complete this analogy:
Plato is to Socrates as Vinny Barbarino is to:

a. Horshack

b. Mr. Kotter

c. Rosalie "Hotzie" Totzie

d. Mr. Woodman

It's Been How Long?

According to tradition, which of the following would be the most appropriate gift to give your spouse on your first anniversary?

a

SILK panties

b

CHROME handcuffs

c

divorce PAPERS

d

RUBBER gloves

You Think "Carrie" Had It Bad...

Say your classmates select you as the person who is most like a small, solid raised area of the skin that does not contain pus. What have you just been voted?

a Most "Pustular"

b Most "Papular"

c Most "Popliteal"

d Most "Poplar"

Vinny was a student of Mr. Kotter on TV's "Welcome Back, Kotter,"
just like Plato was a student of Socrates in ancient times.
And even back then, Socrates would end every class with a bad joke
about his uncle Guido from Queens.

Answer 5

C. TRADITIONALLY, GIFTS OF PAPER ARE GIVEN ON THE FIRST WEDDING ANNIVERSARY. OH, AND LOOK WHAT YOU GOT—A RESTRAINING ORDER!

Answer 6

Most "Papular." A small raised area of the skin that does not contain pus is called a papule. But at least they didn't say you were most like a smushy blood-filled organ in the abdomen and name you the Homecoming Spleen.

My Cousin Vasectomy

Who of the following is MOST likely to lose a loved one
to "pneumoconiosis"?

a. "The Preacher's Wife™"

b. "The Butcher's Wife"

c. "The Monkey's Uncle"

d. "The Coal Miner's Daughter™"

Question 8

UH-oh, hE'S A ConNER!

How did an "Ale Conner" make his money in the Middle Ages?

a. selling imaginary beer

b. holding up liquor shoppes

c. testing the King's ale for poison

d. sitting in a puddle of beer

Question 9

This Looks Like a Job for Ty-D-Bowl™ Man!

If Batman™ keeps the streets of Gotham clean and
Superman™ cleans villains off the streets of Metropolis, what would you
expect a superhero named Voban™ to clean?

a. hair-clogged shower drains

b. puke-puddled grammar school hallways

c. blood-stained hospital sheets

d. wax-filled ears

d. Pneumoconiosis, also known as black lung,
is a common illness among coal miners. Fortunately it's not hereditary,
or else Loretta Lynn would sound more like Joe Cocker.

Answer 8

d. An Ale Conner would sit in a beer puddle for 30 minutes. If his
pants stuck to the seat, the beer had too much sugar and was thrown
away. Who says college doesn't prepare you for the real world?

Answer 9

b. Voban™ is the brand name of that sawdust stuff they sprinkle
in the hallways of grammar schools when kids get sick.

Voban™! Able to absorb partially digested bologna
sandwiches in a single sweep!

I Think,
Therefore I Shoot People

Philosopher or TV Detective?

1. Camus

2. Kojak

3. Mike Hammer

4. Kierkegaard

5. Banacek

6. Jung

7. John Locke

I've Got Your Tragic End Right Here, Baby

killed in gunfight

dies under train

eats dirt

new look

2. Romeo

3. Captain Ahab

shot with mistletoe   adulteress

heart attack

4. Anna Karenina

"Lara's Theme"

trampled by Lamb of God

the whale is God

bubonic plague

poisons himself

never dies

drowns

killed in 'Nam

nailed to cross

1. Doctor Zhivago

amputated leg

beheaded

killed by Doomsday

Just die already!

burns to death

elephant stampede

food poisoning

Pop Rocks™ & Coke™

5. Balder

eats kryptonite™

6. John the Baptist

drug overdose

7. Superman™

boring as hell

DisOrDat Answers

1. Camus/*philosopher*

2. Kojak/*detective*

3. Mike Hammer/*detective*

4. Kierkegaard/*philosopher*

5. Banacek/*detective*

6. Jung/*philosopher*

7. John Locke/*philosopher*

Jack Attack Answers

1. Doctor Zhivago/heart attack

2. Romeo/poisons himself

3. Captain Ahab/drowns

4. Anna Karenina/dies under train

5. Balder/shot with mistletoe

6. John the Baptist/beheaded

7. Superman™/killed by Doomsday

Rate Your Score

36 points or better: Congratulations.
You've won nothing.

30–35 points: Almost perfect.
Hey, even Einstein got some things wrong . . . like that haircut.

20–29 points: Unimpressive.
Sorry, didn't mean to remind you about your life right now.

10–19 points: You tried.
But a trained monkey could've done better.

0–9 points: Just move on.
For you, we wouldn't even have to train the monkey.

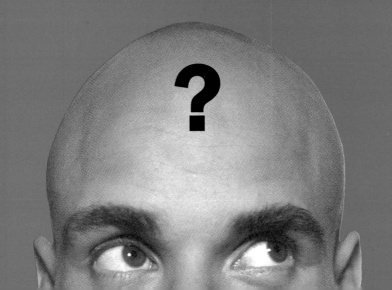

Game

8

Question 1
God Save the Strange, New Government

If the British Parliament finally decided to dissolve the monarchy and replace it with a "menarche" instead, to what would the British population swear allegiance?

a. a Tasmanian aphrodisiac
b. a South American monkey
c. a large wooden boat
d. a woman's first menstruation

Question 2
How'd You Like To Raise My Barn?

The Amish man sitting next to you at the singles bar swears that he's not married. How do you know he's lying?

a. He's wearing black.
b. He's wearing a hat.
c. He has a beard.
d. He's got a cellular phone.

Question 3
Annoying Skinny Guys

Steve Urkel is your typical 98-pound weakling. But what would he be in England?

a. a two-stone weakling
b. a five-stone weakling
c. a seven-stone weakling
d. an 11-meter weakling

Answer 1

A woman's first menstruation is referred to as a menarche.
Either way, Britain's left with a bloody mess.

Answer 2

C. AMISH MEN SHAVE WHILE THEY'RE SINGLE, THEN WHEN THEY GET MARRIED THEY GROW A BEARD. EVEN IF HE DOESN'T HAVE A BEARD, THOUGH, BE CAREFUL. ALL THOSE AMISH GUYS WANT IS TO GET YOU IN THE BACK OF THEIR BUGGY FOR A LITTLE ROLL IN THE HAY.

Answer 3

c. One stone equals 14 pounds, so, in England,
Urkel is a seven-stone weakling. And that's the only time that Urkel
and anything associated with the word "rocks" will be used
in the same sentence.

Question 4
GuYS whO TALk To TheiR DoGS

If Charlie Brown™'s head is a perfect circle with a radius of two inches, what is the diameter of his head?

a.

one inch

b.

two inches

c.

four inches

d.

eight inches

Question 5
Sex, Lies, & Androgyny

You're watching a play in which a character makes people fall in love, but sometimes it's with the wrong people. Suddenly he's whacked with a wooden stick. What are you probably watching?

a. the NHL™'s "A Midsummer Night's Dream"

b. "Peter Pan" performed by flagellants

c. a drum corps doing "Swan Lake"

d. "Cop Rock™"

Gibberish Question 6
It's like a Different Language

Think song lyrics and figure out what line from a popular song this phrase rhymes with:

Never be muddy. Hang dung to right.

Hint **1**

It's from a peppy '80s tune.

Hint **2**

The band is telling you to enjoy your evening.

Hint **3**

Everybody have fun tonight!

C

Four inches. The radius of a circle is always half the diameter. Check out the new back-to-school TV special: "It's the Pythagorean Theorem, Charlie Brown™"

THE NHL™'S "A MIDSUMMER NIGHT'S DREAM." THE PERSON WHO MAKES THE WRONG PEOPLE FALL IN LOVE IN THE SHAKESPEARE PLAY IS CALLED PUCK. THE NHL™ ALREADY HAS PLANS IN PLACE FOR NEXT YEAR'S PRODUCTION, "THE NUTCRACKER."

Gibberish Answer 6

EveRybODY "wanG CHung" ToNiGHT.

Talk about irony. The gibberish phrase makes more sense than the actual answer.

Question 7

El Dorado? Why Don't You Come to Your Senses?

If you drive your Cadillac™ El Dorado to the mythical Latin American city of "El Dorado," what can you bring back in the trunk of your car as a souvenir?

- **a** gold and jewels
- **b** women warriors
- **c** bad weather
- **d** corn chips

Question 8

A MODERN ENGLISH LESSON

"I'll stop the world and melt with you."

In the above line from the '80s hit by Modern English, in which case is the pronoun "you" being used?

- **a** possessive case
- **b** objective case
- **c** nominative case
- **d** hopeless case

Question 9

ANCient GOds & BEaN DiP

If the mythological gods of Greece and Rome were at a mixer, who is the only Greek god who might run into his Roman counterpart wearing the exact same name tag?

a. Dionysus, god of wine

b. Hades, god of the underworld

c. Hermes, messenger of the gods

d. Apollo, god of beauty

A. EL DORADO IS THE NAME OF A MYTHI-CAL LATIN AMERICAN CITY FILLED WITH RICHES. BUT FORGET THE GOLD AND JEWELS—YOU DON'T WANT TO SCRATCH THE PAINT JOB ON YOUR SWEET, SWEET RIDE. THERE'S YOUR GOLD, MY FRIEND.

Answer 8

The pronoun "you" is being used in the objective case in this sentence, because it is the object of the preposition "with." Never thought that song could bother you even more, did you?

Answer 9

Both the Roman and Greek gods of beauty are named Apollo. And, ooh, how embarrassing—they both showed up in the same designer toga.

Are You Eating All Right?
Third World Country or Supermodel?

1. Mozambique

2. Tanzania

3. Tatjana Patitz

4. Burkina Faso

5. Frederique

6. Rwanda

7. Iman

One Good Spin Deserves Another

1. "The Jeffersons™"

"Gimme a Break"

3. "Gomer Pyle, U.S.M.C."

"Diff'rent Strokes™"

"CHiPS"   *"Kiss my grits!"*

"Growing Pains"

boarding school

5. "Flo"

"Well, go-o-ol-ly!"

"The Six Million Dollar Man™"

6. "The Bionic Woman™"

"Night Court™"

"Cheers™"   *"Alice"*

"Wonder Woman™"

Tootie

"The Andy Griffith Show™"

"Mel's Diner"

2. "Fish"

"Amen"

"Sanford & Son™"

"The Goober Show"

"Rhoda"

"Petticoat Junction"

4. "The Sanford Arms"

"Honky"

"Beverly Hills 90210™"

"Barney Miller"

"The Sanford Legs"

"Happy Days™"

7. "The Facts of Life™"

"All in the Family™"

"Oh, Blair!"

1. Mozambique/*country*

2. Tanzania/*country*

3. Tatjana Patitz/*supermodel*

4. Burkina Faso/*country*

5. Frederique/*supermodel*

6. Rwanda/*country*

7. Iman/*supermodel*

Jack Attack Answers

1. "The Jeffersons™"/"All in the Family™"

2. "Fish"/"Barney Miller"

3. "Gomer Pyle, U.S.M.C."/"The Andy Griffith Show™"

4. "The Sanford Arms"/"Sanford & Son™"

5. "Flo"/"Alice"

6. "The Bionic Woman™"/"The Six Million Dollar Man™"

7. "The Facts of Life™"/"Diff'rent Strokes™"

36 points or better:
Fantabulous!

30–35 points:
Extravagantual!

20–29 points:
Amazinacious!

10–19 points:
Spectaculaborous!

0–9 points:
Triumphantastic!

This rating scale brought to you by boxing promoter Don King.

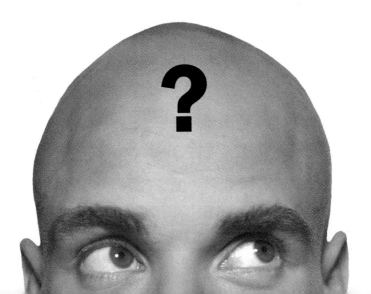

Game

9

THINK WHEN YOU DRINK™

Which of these could you pour into a glass and chug and still rightly claim you're drinking alcohol?

a.
uric acid

b.
cholesterol

c.
insulin

d.
bile

24 Hours of Culinary Delight

Which has never been a dish on Denny's™ menu?

a
Scram Slam™

b
Senior Belgian Waffle Slam™

c
Moons over My Hammy™

d
Paj-Ham-A Party™

Gibberish Question 3
Kiss My Grits, Jack, & Doncha Come Back No More!

With what does this phrase rhyme?
Flo's lover? Me. You're hiking.

Hint 1
It's a safety warning.

Hint 2
You find it on the front of matchbooks.

Hint 3
Shut the lid before lighting it.

Answer 1

Cholesterol is a type of sterol, which is chemically classified as an alcohol. Unless you're under 21, in which case you can only be served Olestra™.

Answer 2

Paj-Ham-A Party! It's not a dish at Denny's™. They don't even have pigs in blankets. Can't a person get a good pork product with a bedtime motif anymore?

Answer 3

CLoSE COVeR BefoRE STRiKinG.

Yeah, because the last thing you want to do when you're smoking is, you know, hurt yourself.

Cocaine & Astrology

If Aquarius were a drug dealer, which sign of the zodiac would he ask for help
if he needed to weigh three grams of coke?

a. Libra
b. Capricorn
c. Aries
d. Scorpio

On the Seventh Day, God Caught a Movie

How could this movie trailer end?

"He's been robbed of his wealth. His children are dead. His skin is covered in boils.
All because his God has made a little bet with Satan. His faith is being tested."

a. Charles Bronson has "The Mark of Cain."
b. Jean-Claude Van Damme is "Risen."
c. Steven Seagal has "The Patience of Job."
d. Chuck Norris is "The Prodigal Son."

Woody Woodchucker

**How much wood would a woodchuck chuck if a woodchuck
could chuck a cord of wood?**

a. 10 knots
b. 25 logarithms
c. 128 cubic feet
d. 250 cubic feet

Answer 5

answer 5 answer 5 answer 5

C. STEVEN SEAGAL HAS "THE PATIENCE OF JOB." IN THE BOOK OF JOB, GOD ALLOWS SATAN TO TORTURE JOB BY DESTROYING HIS LIFE IN ORDER TO PROVE THAT HE HAS FAITH. THE TEST AUDIENCE DIDN'T LIKE IT. SO IN THE HOLLYWOOD VERSION, JOB HAS A BEAUTIFUL WIFE, HEALTHY CHILDREN, AND JUST A SMALL CASE OF ADULT ACNE.

answer 5 answer 5

Answer 6

C. A CORD IS 128 CUBIC FEET OF WOOD. THAT'S A LOT OF WOOD. WHICH LEADS TO THE NEXT QUESTION: HOW MUCH WOOD WOULD A WOODCHUCK UPCHUCK?

Mom, I Don't Want Horseshoes for Breakfast!

If Lucky the Leprechaun™ used technical terms to list the different marshmallows in Lucky Charms™, which of these would NOT be included?

a. pink, hollow muscular organs

b. yellow, crystallized carbon gems

c. orange, gaseous celestial bodies

d. green, leafy leguminous herbs

YOU DID WHAT WITH THAT CANDLESTICK?

Colonel Mustard says he was in four rooms the night of the murder. Which one is he lying about?

a the billiard room

b the hall

c the kitchen

d the den

PASS THE SYRUP, GENGHIS

You're traveling through Mongolian Siberia when you get a craving for flapjacks. Based on the name of the inhabitants' structures, you probably won't find an IHOP™, but you might find a what?

a. International Wigwam of Pancakes

b. International Hogan of Pancakes

c. International Yurt of Pancakes

d. International Wickiup of Pancakes

There are no yellow crystallized carbon gems, or yellow diamonds, in a box of Lucky Charms™—the diamonds are blue. And here's some free advice for General Mills™: don't ever add rabbit's feet to raise cereal sales.

Answer 8

d

The den. There's no den in the Clue™ mansion. There is, however, a study. And it still stinks from the last game when Peacock used the knife to cut the Mustard.

Answer 9

c. A Yurt is a portable tent used by the nomads. Apparently, they have a delicious Rooty, Tooty, Fresh and Sheepy breakfast special.

Is There a "Dr. No" in the House?

Bond™ Film or Medical Ailment?

1. Cauliflower Ear™

2. Goldeneye™

3. Thunderball™

4. Pinkeye™

5. Goldfinger™

6. Octopussy™

7. Black Lung™

It's What's Inside That Count

1. Trojan Horse

egg roll

fortune

rabbit

3. Cracker Jacks™

candy

Helen

three-bean salad

soldiers

5. jumping bean

larva

organs

evils

fiesta

secret toy surprise

baseball games

crackers

pie

rice

spring

2. magician's hat

23 clowns

vegetable

4. fortune cookie

dessert

fruit filling

condoms

lava

6. piñata

wasps

Pandora

7. Pandora's Box

cricket

1. **Cauliflower Ear**/*ailment*

2. **Goldeneye**™/*Bond*™ *film*

3. **Thunderball**™/*Bond*™ *film*

4. **Pinkeye**/*ailment*

5. **Goldfinger**™/*Bond*™ *film*

6. **Octopussy**™/*Bond*™ *film*

7. **Black Lung**/*ailment*

Jack Attack Answers

1. Trojan Horse/soldiers

2. magician's hat/rabbit

3. Cracker Jacks™/secret toy surprise

4. fortune cookie/fortune

5. jumping bean/larva

6. piñata/candy

7. Pandora's Box/evils

36 points or better: Pretty good.
*You need to work
on your posture, though.*

30–35 points: Alright.
*It goes to show you don't have
to be attractive to know things.*

20–29 points: Average.
*You don't always dress that way,
do you?*

10–19 points: Almost respectable.
*Perhaps the circus needs
a new sideshow performer.*

0–9 points: Sad.
You call that a hairdo?

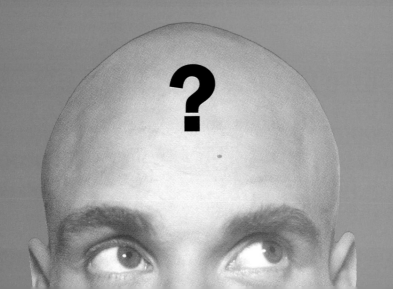

Game

10

Scooby Doo™ & Vitamins

**What's the best name for a new Scooby Doo™ character
who suffers from Vitamin C deficiency?**

- a) Scummy Doo
- b) Rickety Doo
- c) Deficiency Doo
- d) Scurvy Doo

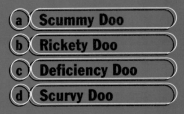

My Head Is Spinning

**If sitcoms were single-celled organisms,
the process of creating a spin-off would be called what?**

a. peristalsis

b. mitosis

c. celodivesis

d. cloning

Iconoclastic Toys

Suppose a leading toy manufacturer decides to cash in
on the Sunday-schooler market and release a new line of biblical toys.
Which baby doll might include a woven-bulrush carrying case?

a. Isaac

b. Jesus

c. Moses

d. Huey

Answer 1

D. SCURVY DOO WOULD BE APPROPRIATE FOR A DOG LACKING VITAMIN C. YOU KNOW, IT WOULD REALLY THROW THE CARTOON WORLD INTO TURMOIL IF SCURVY DOO STARTED TAKING FLINTSTONES™ VITAMINS.

Answer 2

Mitosis is the process where one cell divides into two independent cells. It's not a flawless process. Take the "Happy Days™" cell. Sometimes you get a healthy new cell, like "Laverne & Shirley™." Other times you get a defective mutant, like "Joanie Loves Chachi."

Answer 3

According to the story, Moses was sent adrift in a bulrush basket by his mother and was found by Egyptian princesses.

"The Baby Moses doll! It's safe to use near water, and it's guaranteed to last over 900 years! (Stone tablets sold separately.)"

Question 4
ASS-TroNOmiCaL ProPORtionS

If the Roman god Mercury, the Venus de Milo and your anus suddenly ballooned to the size of the planets Mercury, Venus, and Uranus, which of these series would be true?

a.
big god, medium butt hole, small statue

b.
big god, medium statue, small butt hole

c.
big butt hole, medium statue, small god

d.
big butt hole, medium god, small statue

Question 5
THE PERIODIC TABLE OF POOR TASTE

Everybody knows that H_2O is water and CO_2 is carbon dioxide, but take a look at this:

Which of the following "words" is NOT formed from actual symbols for atomic elements?

a. Sh-Lo-Ng
b. Cr-O-Tc-H
c. Te-S-Ti-Cl-Es
d. Ba-Co-N

Gibberish Question 6
Those Damn Yuppies & Their Campaign Slogans

With what song title does this phrase rhyme?
Flaky yuppie "Gore, too!" logo.

Hint 1
It's a repetitive '80s tune.

Hint 2
The song is about getting up in the morning.

Hint 3
Wake up!

c. Big butt hole, medium statue, small god. Uranus, the planet, is the third largest in our solar system. Venus is the fourth smallest and Mercury is the second smallest. Look at it this way. You won't even feel it when someone has to take your temperature.

Sh, Lo, and Ng are NOT symbols for atomic elements. Ain't learnin' fun?

Gibberish Answer 6

"Wake Me Up Before You Go-Go"

Ever wonder where that other guy from Wham! went-went?

Stark Raving Mad & Smarter than Everyone Else

If René Descartes and Andre the Giant were combined into one person, which of these sayings might have been coined?

a. No man is a faulty thyroid gland unto himself.

b. The half Nelson is mightier than the sword.

c. I think, therefore I slam.

d. Time keeps on ticking into the turnbuckle.

ThE NUdiTY & thE PapaCY

The Pope is undressing to take a soak in a hot tub. If he removes his hat first, which vestment will he be removing?

a.
the chasuble

b.
the cassock

c.
the rochet

d.
the miter

SNACKS WE'RE COMPLETELY NUTS OVER

Which of the following was a real candy sold in the U.S.?

a. Charlie Chimp's Chocolate Cherries

b. Chocolate-Covered Gorilla Balls

c. Gopher Gonads

d. Honey-Roasted Condors' Nuts

I think, therefore I slam. René "The Giant" Descartes, the world's first philosopher-wrestler, wouldn't just pin you, he'd convince the referee that he didn't exist and then knee you in the balls.

Answer 8

The miter is the Pope's big honkin' hat. So he's got the Popemobile. Do you think they call his bath tub the Popetub . . . or perhaps the Popeshower?

Answer 9

B. CHOCOLATE-COVERED GORILLA BALLS. THEY WERE MALTED MILK BALLS. AND NO, THEY WERE NOT SOLD IN A WRINKLY BAG.

Forsooth, I Ache!

Shakespearean Play or Disease?

1. Cirrhosis

2. Syphilis

3. Troilus & Cressida

4. Titus Andronicus

5. Gingivitis

6. Coriolanus

7. Dermatitis

Death by & with Chocolate

1. Goobers™

coconut

gooey

peanut butter

peanuts

almonds

raisins   *geeks*

4. Mounds™

5. Mars Bar™

malted milk

salty   *sweet*   *kiwi*

7. Whoppers™

cookie

boogers

candy

BUN™

. . . don't.

2. Reeses™

bananas

chipped beef

3. Raisinettes™

snot

chicken

movie food

mole

tuna fish

cherries

grasshoppers

Almond Joy™

6. Twix™

yogurt

DisOrDat Answers

1. Cirrhosis/*disease*

2. Syphilis/*disease*

3. Troilus & Cressida/*play*

4. Titus Andronicus/*play*

5. Gingivitis/*disease*

6. Coriolanus/*play*

7. Dermatitis/*disease*

Jack Attack Answers

1. Goobers™/peanuts

2. Reeses™/peanut butter

3. Raisinettes™/raisins

4. Mounds™/coconut

5. Mars Bar™/almonds

6. Twix™/cookie

7. Whoppers™/malted milk

Rate Your Score

36 points or better: Nice.
You look like a million bucks.

30–35 points: Not bad.
You look like twenty bucks.

20–29 points: Mediocre.
*If you save some money, you can have
a shopping spree at the Everything's
A Dollar store.*

10–19 points: Oops.
*You shouldn't have spent eight bucks
on a stupid trivia book when you
could have used it for precious food.*

0–9 points: That's really bad.
You owe us money.

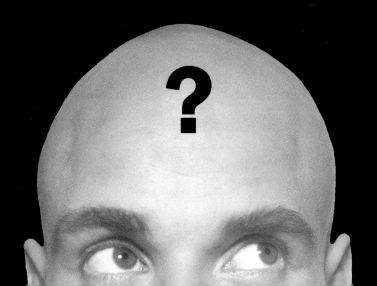

THAT'S IT. NO MORE. You've exhausted all the trivia in this book and maybe, just maybe, you learned a little bit about yourself in the process.

Well, we're not satisfied.

In order to give you the very best value that your $7.95 can buy, here are some ways to extend the life of this book:

- 5½" x 8½" flash cards (white-out the existing text first)
- something to cover carpet stains
- attach wheels and a leash and PRETEND it's a small dog
- booster seat for an exceptionally small child
- use pages as wrapping paper
- in lieu of Mace, smack muggers in the face with it
- BRAIN TEASER: Guess how many pages are in the book. Look at the last page to see if you're right. Repeat.
- excellent source of fiber
- flip pages and make bets with friends on whether or not the word "BUTT" will appear on the page
- give yourself a refreshing paper cut
- handy TOE SEPARATOR for use when applying toenail polish
- oven mitt
- hummingbird landing pad
- paste photos and newspaper clippings into it for a scrapbook
- fun tool for obedience-training your dog
- individual pages make handy CHRISTMAS TREE ORNAMENTS
- a kite for EXTREMELY windy days
- completely ineffective flip book
- MARITAL AID
- take to pawn shop, trade for enough to buy half a phone call
- combine with sticks and mud for this winter's nest
- throw out window for experiment in gravity
- weight for your light forearm exercises
- air freshener (SCENT NOT INCLUDED)